THE PRICE OF JUSTICE IN AMERICA

Commentaries on the Criminal Justice System and Ways to Fix What's Wrong

by Paul Brakke

THE PRICE OF JUSTICE IN AMERICA

Copyright © 2016 by Paul Brakke

All rights reserved. No part of this book may be used or reproduced by any means, graphic, electronic, or mechanical, including photocopying, recording, taping or by any information storage retrieval system without the written permission of the author except in the case of brief quotations embodied in critical articles and reviews.

TABLE OF CONTENTS

INTRODUCTION 7
PART I: THE RISING RACIAL TENSIONS IN AMERICA 9
CHAPTER 1: OVERCOMING THE POLICE-CITIZEN DIVIDE 11
   The Number of Citizens Killed by the Police 12
   Some Ways to Improve Citizen-Police Relationships 14
CHAPTER 2: REFLECTIONS ON RACISM IN AMERICA 15
   The Fears Underlying Racism 15
   Fixing the System 18
PART II: PROBLEMS IN THE PRISON SYSTEM 21
CHAPTER 3: WHY PRISONS TODAY ARE CONTRIBUTING TO AMERICA GOING BROKE 23
   The Extent of the Problem 23
   Some Possible Solutions 25
CHAPTER 4: AN EXAMPLE OF A SUCCESSFUL PRISON PROGRAM 27
CHAPTER 5: FAMILIES ARE COLLATERAL DAMAGE DUE TO THE HIGH INCARCERATION RATE 31
   The Forgotten Families 32
   Reducing the Collateral Damage 34
PART III: HOMICIDE PATTERNS IN DIFFERENT COMMUNITIES AND GROUPS 37
CHAPTER 6: THE REAL TRUTH ABOUT BLACK AND WHITE HOMICIDE RATES IN AMERICA 39
   Five Key Truths about Homicide Patterns in America 40
   Some Startling Conclusions about Homicide in America 43

CHAPTER 7: HOW BAD ARE BLACK HOMICIDE RATES? 45
The Major Correlations 45
How I Made the Correlations 47
Other Correlations for Violent Crime Rates 48
What These Correlations Show about Crime 49

CHAPTER 8: WHY ARE URBAN BLACKS ASSOCIATED WITH VIOLENT CRIME? 51
Results of the Analysis 52
Reasons for the Results 52

CHAPTER 9: REDUCING VIOLENT CRIME BY RELIEVING BLACK URBAN POVERTY 55
The Role of Role Models 56
Some Conclusions and Suggestions 59

CHAPTER 10: HISPANIC CONTRIBUTIONS TO VIOLENT CRIME 61
What the Correlation Results Show 62
Why the Lack of Correlation? 64

PART IV: HOMICIDE RATES AND DRUGS 65

CHAPTER 11: DRUG OVERDOSES VS. HOMICIDES 67

PART V: HOW THE MEDIA DISTORTS THE NEWS ABOUT CRIME 71

CHAPTER 12: HOW THE MEDIA PROMOTES CONFRONTATIONS AND DISTORTS THE NEWS 73
Some Examples of Distorting the News 74
The Consequences of Misleading Media Accounts 77
Some Suggestions for Reducing Misleading Accounts in the Media 78

CHAPTER 13: WHEN THE MEDIA GOES TOO FAR: COVERING THE TRIAL OF A JUDGE FOR HIS CHILD'S DEATH 79

CHAPTER 14: WAS THERE JUSTICE? THE RANGE OF ATTITUDES REFLECTED BY JUDGE NARAMORE'S TRIAL FOR HIS CHILD'S DEATH 85

    An Overview of the Case 86

    Reactions to the Naramore Case 87

    ABOUT THE AUTHOR 93

INTRODUCTION

THE PRICE OF JUSTICE IN AMERICA features a series of blogs I have written about problems in the criminal justice system and how they might be fixed. I have been writing these blogs for my website (www.americanjusticethebook.com) as a follow-up to my book *American Justice?* These are designed to expand upon issues originally raised in my book or discuss new topics based on recent articles in the news dealing with criminal justice issues.

As these blogs describe, the criminal justice system is beset by problems due to a number of factors. These include racial tensions, especially between African-Americans and the police and difficulties in the prison system, due to the high cost of incarceration, higher conviction rates and longer sentences for minority groups, and a high recidivism rate, in part because those released have barriers to finding jobs and a good income doing legitimate work because of their sentence. Other problems have been caused by the ongoing War on Drugs and the large number of prisoners, mostly individuals of color, who are there for non-violent, largely drug-related, offenses. Still other problems are the high homicide rates, primarily in the inner cities and much of it black on black killings, often linked to battles over territory by gangs. And then the media contributes to these problems with its sensational and often misleading or factually incorrect news. In fact, some recent news stories have discussed the problem of "fake news."

In this first collection of blogs, I have dealt with these various issues, and in some cases suggested what to do to fix the problem. My hope is that the chapters featuring these blogs will contribute to the ongoing discussion about what is wrong in the system and what to do to fix it.

These suggestions should be especially timely in light of the elections with not only a new President nationally, but new officials in Congress and the state level. Among them will be individuals who are especially interested in criminal justice issues, and it is my hope that the blogs in this book, as well as my original book *American Justice?* will help to inform the ongoing discussion about the system and what to do to improve it.

The chapters are divided into the following sections:
- the rising racial tensions, especially between the police and the black community
- problems in the prison and correctional system
- differences in the homicide rate in different communities and groups
- the way drug overdoses dwarf homicide rates
- the role of the media in sensationalizing crime and contributing to problems in the criminal justice system

PART I: THE RISING RACIAL TENSIONS IN AMERICA

CHAPTER 1: OVERCOMING THE POLICE-CITIZEN DIVIDE

Almost every day, the media features another case of a citizen being killed by the police, and some cases this coverage results in a storm of protests, since community members think the person has been singled out unjustly. It's different when the police kill someone who has killed dozens of innocent people, such as in San Bernardino or Orlando, Florida. But in other cases, such as with the death of Freddie Gray in Baltimore in the back of a police van after a questionable release or in the shooting of Mario Woods in San Francisco, after he slashed a stranger with a knife and was shot 20 times by the police, people think the police were too quick to act. And often people think the victim was killed due to racial profiling, whereby the police are more likely to kill African-Americans than others in these confrontations.

I began look at this growing police-citizen divide after writing *American Justice?*, which includes a discussion of problems in the criminal justice system. I began writing it after my wife had her own difficult encounter, beginning when the police dragged her out of a restaurant to arrest her. They were acting in response to a claim by some neighborhood kids that she had tried to run them over, although this was a false claim, because the kids didn't like her complaining to the police about their unsafe play in the streets. So this was their way of getting back at her. But much as happens in these cases that escalate into the police killing a citizen, the police didn't wait to hear my wife's side of the story. Her arrest occurred in a very public place, and fortunately, it didn't escalate to the point where a police officer pulled out a gun and shot her.

But sometimes, this is how these killings start, such as when a wife or neighbor reports that a man is behaving erratically. Instead of responding by trying to find out what's wrong and calm the man down, once he makes a move that may be wrongly interpreted as a threat to the police, such as reaching into his pocket for a cell phone, the police shoot and ask questions later.

The Number of Citizens Killed by the Police

The number of these civilians killed by police is truly astounding, because the cases that end up in the headlines are only the tip of the iceberg, as I discovered in looking at the statistics. In 2015, 990 people were shot and killed by police, and 258 of them were black. Another 48 blacks were killed by police in some other fashion. Since many of those killed were armed, there may well have been justification for the killings. But of the 305 blacks killed, 102 were unarmed. Only 10 of the cases of killings of unarmed blacks were prosecuted and only 2 of those cases resulted in convictions. There were no murder convictions.

Most of the killings were in urban areas. That's because in these confrontations, the police approach the suspect with a siege mentality, given the already hostile relationships between the police and the community in these areas. Thus, they are more ready to feel threatened and shoot, whereas if they encounter a white man who is mentally disturbed or drunk, they are more likely to try to talk to him and diffuse the situation.

In turn, such shootings of people of color has contributed to even more hostility to the police in the inner city and among African-Americans – and to still more headlines, inflaming the situation even more. This is not to say that in some cases, such as in facing down a terrorist who has shot down dozens of victims, the police are not justified in killing the suspect, and then people are gratified they have killed. But in many other cases, the police could use diplomacy and negotiation tactics to calm the suspect, so they can arrest him rather than killing him, and then he will have his day in court.

Some Ways to Improve Citizen-Police Relationships

Thus, as I have discussed in *American Justice?* in proposing ways to fix the criminal justice system, I think there are a number of ways to improve police-citizen relationships, which will contribute to lowering the cost of operating the system, too. For example, additional national training guidelines might be developed for police departments throughout the nation detailing when the police should use force to protect themselves and when they should use other methods to control and subdue the suspect.

The police might also withdraw to a safe distance when a suspect has a knife, so they are not in danger of being attacked at close quarters, which will give them more time to try to cool down the situation. If a suspect is running away, it is better to let that person go and seek to make an arrest later, rather than shoot that person to stop an escape. Also, the participation on local citizen review boards might be expanded by including some members of the local board of supervisors in order to increase community-wide participation and facilitate more citizen and police cooperation. I also think it will help to provide more transparency about police operations, such as by removing any restrictions on members of the public filming and recording the police on duty. These measures will help the police better deal more peaceably with a current situation, while helping to build trust in the community. This approach can reduce costs, too, given the high cost of dealing with the investigation and the legal fallout following any police-citizen killing.

CHAPTER 2: REFLECTIONS ON RACISM IN AMERICA

Let's face it. Racism has been a continuing problem in America, from the days of slavery to today. One result of this continued treatment of most blacks as second class citizens, is continued resentment which occasionally boils over into a confrontation – whether it's one angry black man raging at a white man or a group of angry blacks joining together to protest, loot, trash, or otherwise attack property in the neighborhood.

The Fears Underlying Racism

In turn, many whites fear blacks. This fear wasn't much of a worry during slavery, when black subjugation was total. It became more of an issue since, with other forms of subjugation such as lynching, which lasted another 50 years, followed by a period of intense segregation. Desegregation was never very successful and in fact promoted white flight from the inner cities to the suburbs, leaving the inner cities to become cauldrons of crime involving economically distressed blacks and hispanics.

Whites haven't been too concerned about black-on-black crime, including murder, as long as it didn't spill over into their communities. Police became viewed as the first line of defense to keep whites safe from black crime. Yet the mostly white police had to deal with this crime, risking their lives on the front lines of racial tension -- in minority communities where they often weren't wanted or appreciated, because their tactics were often discriminatory or led to discriminatory consequences.

A prime example is when a police officer is quick to suspect an African-American man who happened to be within a few blocks of where a crime occurred. So the black man becomes a prime suspect whether he closely fits the description of the suspect or not. He was black, too, wasn't he, and the witness could easily have been mistaken, so the police officer's thinking might go. So the innocent black man is soon arrested, and once in the system, he is often misidentified as the perpetrator of the crime and within a few months, convicted of a crime he didn't do. And another key reason for this miscarriage of justice is by having less job opportunities and living in the inner city, he doesn't have the money to get bail or hire a good defense lawyer. Then the system too readily gobbles him up and he joins the disproportionately black prison population, and his only real crime, so to speak, is being "black in America," where he is more likely to be poor, unemployed, and living in an inner city in an environment where drugs, crime, and despair can be found on most city streets everyday.

Periodically, the situation where blacks were continually disadvantaged boiled over into race riots, such as in the sixties. This brought more fear to whites, and the criminal justice system responded with more and more severe sentencing, ballooning the prison system and its associated costs. Some attempts at reform have been implemented locally, such as more community involvement by police, but if the police don't actually live in the neighborhoods they police, it is difficult for them to be accepted by those communities.

Thus, racial tension has continued to be a problem in this country. Witness the events of the past couple of years including the shooting by the cops of Michael Brown in Ferguson, Missouri and Walter Scott in Charleston, South Carolina; the death of Freddie Gray in a police van in Baltimore, Maryland, and most recently the killings of Philando Castille in St. Paul, Minnesota and Alton Steele in Baton Rouge, Louisiana, which finally led to the ambush shooting of cops by Micah Johnson in Dallas, Texas. After a while, the names of the victims and the killers blend together and may be forgotten, with just the city names as monuments to the days of rage and destruction.

For the most part the killings have been done by cops, though recently more and more cops are being killed, about 50 a year in the last decade, but that's still less than one-third of the rate per policeman seen in the 1970s. While there may be many factors at play in causing these killings, a continuing theme is the feelings of anger and fear of the other. The police suspect the black man as up to no good and are more prone to shoot first rather than considering any alternatives, while some angry and alienated black men have been influenced by feelings of injustice to strike back in what is often a certain death following their act.

But even though these are killings by individuals and, it would be a big mistake to attribute the actions of a few rogue police or blacks to police or blacks generally, there is no denying that racial tension contributes to the impetus for killings. And currently, that tension has come to a head in the face-off between cops and African-Americans, whether individual cops and blacks are fighting each other or African-American protesters are sharing their anger with the world. Plus now a growing movement to support the cops – Blue Lives Matter – has emerged from the ashes of the recent cop killing in Dallas. The media often are complicit in tensions, because they contribute to whipping up attention to conflicts. But so are whites who are content to let the situation fester as long as it doesn't directly affect them. Or they go for simple solutions, such as seeking a crackdown based on the slogan: "Let's not get soft on crime!" But they don't realize that the situation is complex, and a crackdown by itself will only provoke more resistance and fiercer battles.

Fixing the System

So, what's the fix? Clearly, just as there's no single cause, there's no one single fix. The situation has festered for decades and only gotten worse. The numbers are truly appalling. According to data from the U.S. Department of Prisons, FBI, Pew Research, and other sources, about 2 million Americans are in federal, state, and county prisons and jails around the country, and the racial disparities are striking. Black men are six times more likely than white men to be in prison, while Hispanic men are 2.4 times more likely to be there. Moreover, 1 out of 31 Americans are under U.S. corrections custody either through parole, probation, or incarceration, and one in three Americans have a criminal record.

But we need to do something, before the racial divide becomes even greater. A comprehensive plan for criminal justice reform is one place to start, and that's what I call for in my book

American Justice?. In these divisive, partisan times, it just could be that this is one issue that conservatives concerned about cost and liberals/progressives concerned about discrimination can finally get together in a long-overdue bipartisan manner to regain some public confidence in Washington, DC.

However, not just lawmakers need to get involved. The public has to get involved as well, and push the lawmakers into action. A national dialogue is called for, where both sides acknowledge their contribution to this sad state of affairs. Instead of pointing fingers to lay blame on the other side for what they allegedly did wrong, individuals on both sides of the issue or the aisle need to listen to one another more, whereby they try to understand how difficult things are for those on the other side.

Racial tension is unlikely to go away anytime soon by legislation alone. But we can embark on a path where it can slowly wind down and recede if there is enough public will to address the root causes of this racial tension. A key part of this solution is to see things from the perspective or the other side, and then try to reform matters. The first step is to become more aware of the way the criminal justice system works. The police and blacks are certainly aware of how it usually operates, but they are often intimidated and scared when they confront each other in any situation, such as when a police officer stops a car for a traffic violation. What may seem routine when a police officer stops a white driver, whether for a broken tail light, lack of registration, improperly changing lanes or speeding, is fraught with the potential for violence when an officer stops a black driver. While the police officer may be fearing the driver may have a gun and reach for it to retaliate, the black driver is already thinking about the other black drivers shot by the police and worried if he might be next if he makes the slightest wrong move. So a simple stop is anything but that.

    Whites who don't encounter the system have to educate themselves about how the system really operates on others who are affected by it everyday, especially in the inner city. Whites have to realize the kind of monstrosity this system has become for-inner city residents and recognize their own role in creating this system which may operate well for them but has disastrous consequences for others. We all need to realize what is going on before anyone can hope to reform or fix the system with a goal of ending the division and the fear it brings. So now it's time to start before the monster of a system we have created gets any worse!

PART II: PROBLEMS IN THE PRISON SYSTEM

CHAPTER 3: WHY PRISONS TODAY ARE CONTRIBUTING TO AMERICA GOING BROKE

Since writing *American Justice?*, I've been following some of the recent news on how costly and ineffective the American prison system really is. The cost is over $70 billion each year, and when you consider the high percentage of the population in prison and not productive members of society, you have to consider whether there is a way to reduce these costs. These cost reductions will also benefit society by reducing the number of prisoners who can be safely released and finding other means of punishment and rehabilitation.

I have become especially concerned about these prison issues, as a result of my own wife's arrest and jailing based on false charges and testimony. Certainly she didn't need to be imprisoned in a mental health facility while these charges were investigated, and that led me to realize how many other prisoners are incarcerated who don't need to be. In fact, hundreds of these prisoners have later been found innocent, after DNA testing and further witness testimony proved they were wrongly convicted.

The Extent of the Problem

Just how big is this problem? Huge. Approximately 1 out of every 32 Americans – about 7.2 million adults -- are on probation, on parole, or in prison at any given time. This total includes 2.3 million Americans in prison, nearly one in every hundred adults. In fact, the U.S. has the highest rate of incarceration in the world, since more Americans per capita are in prison than in other countries. Though America has 5% of the world's population, 25% of the world's prisoners are here.

When you think about it, the costs of imprisonment are astronomical, since not only is there the cost of building the prisons and hiring the security personnel to run them, but most prisoners could be productive members of society if released. So there is a huge cost to society for keeping them in prison. Plus there are costs for the prisoners' families, given the loss of a provider, which sometimes means losing a home because of not being able to afford the mortgage or rent anymore.

To put some numbers on the costs, these amount to over $70 billion annually in the U.S., with the result that state governments, which are responsible for most prisons, are increasingly strapped. Ironically, the average cost of keeping a prisoner in prison ranges from about $14,000 per inmate in some states to $60,000 in other states. And much of the money goes to privatized prisons, which make up over 10% of the corrections market and earn about $7.4 billion a year, according to a recent article on "The Economics of the American Prison System" by Thierry Godard in SmartAsset.com.

As I describe in my book *American Justice?*, the costs have increased by the growing number of prisoners, because of a number of reasons, including the decline of the middle class due to the growing inequality, leading many once law-abiding citizens to turn to crime. Then, too, many individuals have turned to crime due to the breakdown of many institutions, like the educational system and the church, and they have been influenced by the images of wealth and high living presented on the Internet.

Some Possible Solutions

Whatever the reasons for the increase of crime and incarceration, I'd like to suggest a number of possible solutions to improve the system, which I have described in *American Justice?* One simple way is for judges to reduce the length of sentences. Also, judges can use alternative forms of sentencing, such as halfway houses, home detention, community service, and workfare programs for non-violent offenders. I think that helping ex-cons find meaningful jobs is an especially good way to keep them from returning to crime, since having a job gives them an incentive to stay on the straight and narrow, instead of looking to the criminals they have gotten to know in prison to help them get money from criminal activities.

CHAPTER 4: AN EXAMPLE OF A SUCCESSFUL PRISON PROGRAM

Since writing *American Justice?*, inspired by my wife's nightmarish experience with a punitive criminal justice system and a possible 16-year prison sentence if she didn't accept a plea for us to move and pay some legal costs, I have been looking at new developments in the prisons. Maybe something might help to change the grim statistics which show high incarceration rates that show the U.S. has more prisoners per capita than any other country – nearly 1 out of every 100 adults, about 2.3 million Americans.

For most prisoners, even if they get out, being incarcerated is like a life sentence, in that being branded a felon makes it more difficult if not impossible to get a good job, resulting in a struggle to survive that leads many back to crime. Then, too, for most prisoners, the experience is like being in a warehouse, with little or no learning, so any useful skills can be lost – another reason it can be hard to find a job.

However, a recent *Time* magazine article in the July 11-18 issue provides an example of another model for offering prisoners help and hope, which can turn them into useful citizens again, thereby reducing the costs to society. Essentially, this prison, San Quentin, located in Marin County near San Rafael, offers a series of programs where prisoners can get therapy, take educational courses, and learn new jobs. As the article points out, over 90% of prisoners eventually do return to society, so it makes sense to help them learn the skills and self-control they need to follow the law when they get out. The problem with most prisons is that they offer at most a high school GED and training in manual labor, and they are located in remote areas, so prisoners can readily get disconnected from members of their family, who could be a vital link to helping them reintegrate with society.

But San Quentin is different. Out of about 4000 prisoners, it has about 3000 participants in various programs it offers. Among other things, the participants get therapy on overcoming their addictions or on managing their anger. They can gain writing and communications experience by working on the prison newspaper or radio station. They can take college courses. Especially useful is a program where they learn software-engineering skills and even earn a little money by writing code for companies in the Silicon Valley, which enables them to have the needed skills to be employed in the high-tech job market when they are released. By 2017, the program hopes to enroll 200 participants at four California prisons, and then involve prisons outside the state.

The results of these kinds of programs are promising, since studies suggest that prisoners who participate are less likely to return to prison, presumably because they are committing less or no crimes. Thus, this is a model that offers hope not only for the prisoners who go through these programs but for the prison system, the state, and the taxpayers who foot the bill, by reducing the costs of incarceration.

In *American Justice?*, I suggest a number of other solutions for improving the criminal justice system, from the actions of the police and the courts to corrections. This is one more useful approach I would add to the solutions I suggest.

CHAPTER 5: FAMILIES ARE COLLATERAL DAMAGE DUE TO THE HIGH INCARCERATION RATE

I have recently been paying attention to the media coverage of crime and have become aware of how really distorted the information we get from the media truly is. A case in point is the lack of stories about families in trouble due to incarceration of a loved one, whereas the big story is about the crime, the conviction, and the killer. By contrast, there are few stories about the victims or the families of the incarcerated defendants, unless they happen to be famous, such as when a celebrity is killed or a TV star goes to prison, such as Teresa Guidice of *The Real Housewives of New Jersey* and *Celebrity Apprentice.* A series of *People* magazine articles and other news articles have featured their story, describing how she spent 11 months in prison and now stays home with the kids while her husband serves a 41 month sentence, both for bankruptcy fraud, though their jail sentences were split so they could each spend time at home caring for their kids.

The problem is that the media plays up the drama of police arrests and convictions, and once a defendant or victim is well-known, their story is what is featured in the news. Likewise, the protests that erupt over especially egregious police actions receive a lot of media attention, particularly when these protests might turn violent.

The Forgotten Families

Forgotten in this media and public attention are the families of the victims or the convicted and incarcerated defendant. The justice system offers only some sympathy to victims' families, and certainly none to defendants' families, though family stability and values provide the backbone for a strong society. These families are the forgotten casualties of the criminal justice system, as I describe at more length in my book *American Justice?*, which deals with the many problems in the criminal justice system and how to fix them.

In my view, these family victims represent "collateral damage." It's a term commonly used to refer to the unintended damages from a military operation, which includes the destruction of civilians. This term fits the family of a prisoner, too, because whenever a family member is incarcerated or killed, there can be great damage to family units – including spouses, children, parents, and relatives, and all of the defendant's or victim's relationships. Stories of murders generally focus on the investigation and defendants, who are impacted negatively at all stages of a prosecution, from the initial charge to the trial and verdict. But what happens to their family members is largely ignored by the media and public.

Unfortunately, these damages can be huge and lifelong. I became especially sensitive to this issue, when I became collateral damage after my wife was falsely accused by some kids in the neighborhood of trying to run one of them over. She had to endure being thrown into a psych ward for a five day evaluation and then a series of hearings, forcing her to finally accept a plea bargain, whereby we had to move out of the neighborhood and sell our house at a loss. Meanwhile, through this long exhausting process, I suffered extensively along with her. As I wrote in my book: "I felt her anger. I felt her despair...And there was nothing I seemed to be able to do to protect her, which made me feel inadequate and worthless." My relationships at work deteriorated, too, since colleagues had trouble understanding what I was experiencing, and I, as well as my wife, experienced a lack of privacy when the local media picked up the story. In addition, my wife has never been the same, and the damage to our family's finances became extensive and excessive.

While my wife and I just barely had the finances to weather the storm, many families of defendants and victims don't, especially when they are already living in the inner city where much of the crime violence that affects both victims and defendants occurs. Thus, when a male who has been the major family provider is killed or sent to prison, the family may become financially unstable. The wife may not make enough with a single income to pay the bills, and other relatives and friends may not be in a position to help. So after a few months or perhaps a year, the family may end up losing its home or be unable to pay the rent and end up living in a car, van, or truck, or worse – reduced to living in a tent. Some of the cities with a high homeless population, such as

San Francisco and Oakland, have found that a large percentage – about a quarter to a third of the homeless population – was formerly part of the middle or working class and until recently had homes. But then, due to an unlucky break, such as having a main provider incarcerated or the victim of a crime, they ended up as a homeless statistic.

In *American Justice?*, I have described at length the problems that these families encounter – from financial woes to the breakdown of the family and the end of personal relationships for an individual who is incarcerated. Moreover, the children may suffer lasting damage, finding it difficult to cope with a parent's incarceration or death due to a violent crime.

Reducing the Collateral Damage

What is the solution to help reduce the collateral damage? In *American Justice?* and in further researching the problem, I have come up with a number of possible solutions to deal with the collateral damage these families of prisoners suffer. One approach is to provide extra counseling, tutoring and mentoring support through the schools to the children of incarcerated parents. Support programs could be established for the wives and children of returning prisoners, much like for the families of returning soldiers to help them better know and adjust to the difficulties ahead. Also, the partners of prisoners could form small support groups to take care of each other's children when at work or during prison visits. Additionally, I recommend the expansion of re-entry and job training for prisoners and ex-prisoners to help them successfully enter normal society. All of these programs can be provided at a low cost to reduce the collateral damage problem, while helping the families become more productive members of society. In my view, these approaches can be a win-win for both the prisoners and their families and for society as a whole.

PART III: HOMICIDE PATTERNS IN DIFFERENT COMMUNITIES AND GROUPS

CHAPTER 6: THE REAL TRUTH ABOUT BLACK AND WHITE HOMICIDE RATES IN AMERICA

Recently, the shootings of blacks by police and the retaliatory shootings of the police by blacks around the U.S. has become a crisis. Certainly there is very little justification for killings of unarmed citizens by police. The only justification is whether the police officer is concerned that his or her own life might be in jeopardy when making a split-second decision about whether to shoot or not. The Black Lives Matter movement has been swift to condemn individual police shootings of blacks and to organize protests. An All Lives Matter movement has arisen in response to say that every life should be treated as worthwhile. Both sides have their points, but they don't seem to try to reconcile these perspectives to arrive at any consensus about what should be done.

Contributing to the misunderstandings that have furthered this crisis, the media has placed much emphasis on individual events that have involved mass killings. In response, gun-control advocates and others have raised the issue of whether assault weapons should be restricted. Predictably, the National Rifle Association has claimed that liberals are trying to restrict gun ownership.

But what do the homicide statistics show rather than just looking at individual cases? These present a very different picture of what is going on, although in looking at these statistics, I have taken a different approach from the individual examples I used to make points in the chapters of my book *American Justice?*, published recently by TouchPoint Press. When I looked at these homicide statistics, I found a number of shocking facts.

Five Key Truths about Homicide Patterns in America

First and foremost, 1.4 million deaths by firearm occurred between 1968 and 2011, a horrible number by any account. However, this number of deaths is not the worst in the world. Our per capita homicide rate is not as bad as that of Russia, Mexico, or many Central American, South American or African countries.

Second, what isn't widely known given the media emphasis

on reporting murders, guns account for more suicides than homicides. Out of 33,000 annual deaths caused by guns, 22,000 were suicides, about two-thirds of the deaths by guns, while only 8600 were homicides. Another 2500 were accidents or unintentional. Unfortunately, restricting guns is unlikely to significantly decrease the number of suicides, since those who are intent on ending their lives have so many other methods they can use – from taking pills to jumping off of bridges.

Third, crime statistics show that the vast majority of homicides do not involve assault weapons, even though the police may fear being overwhelmed by the firepower of mass murderers. Over 70% of homicides involve handguns, the very weapon most commonly chosen to protect households from break-ins. Therefore, the only way to make a significant dent on homicide statistics would be to make it more difficult to procure handguns, which are rarely used for hunting or even by militias.

However, this effort is unrealistic, since the NRA would be very likely to fight any attempt to reduce firearms in the country. Citizens in high crime areas would also rebuff any attempt to impose restrictions on their ability to defend themselves.

Therefore, restricting handguns is not likely to be an option to reduce homicides either. In any case, gun ownership in households has actually declined since 1977, from 50% down to 31% as of 2014, and a far greater proportion of households in rural America possess guns (56%) than urban Americans living in large metropolitan areas (16%) with higher crime statistics.

Fourth, in 2014 more murderers were male (4878 or 90%) than female (543 or 10%); just as more murder victims were male (3976 or 70%) than female (1679 or 30%). So murders are mostly males killing males. At the same time, women are three times more likely to be murder victims than murderers.

Fifth, it appears that most homicides occur within racial groups, so that most whites are killed by whites and most blacks are killed by blacks. As the statistics show, in 2014, 2488 of 3021 or 82% white gun homicide victims were killed by whites or Hispanics, while 2205 of 2451 or 90% of black gun homicide victims were killed by blacks. By contrast, only 18% of black homicide victims were killed by whites. Blacks are the true victims, since proportionate to their population, they are 4 times more likely to be murdered than everyone else, and 6.6 times more likely to be killed than whites.

Some Startling Conclusions about Homicide in America

Thus the statistics show that the overwhelming majority of African American homicides are perpetrated by other blacks. Only a very small proportion of black killings (about 250) are carried out by whites, though certainly such killings should be condemned and reduced, too. Only about 100 killings of unarmed blacks are due to the police, though the media and Black Lives Matter movement have made these seem much more frequent and due to out of control police bias against blacks than is really the case.

Similarly, only a very small proportion of white killings are carried out by blacks, and most white deaths are due to white on white crime (about 2500), with involvement by the police in about 500. Maybe that's because we still live in a very segregated society. But, whatever the reason, the key point to recognize is that since most blacks are killed by other blacks, and very few by the police, the Black Lives Matter movement could save far more black lives by looking at making changes within the communities where most blacks live in order to stem the one of the major sources of black on black homicides – gang wars and conflicts between gangs. While statistics on gang related homicide are hard to come by, it has been estimated that nearly half of all violent crime is committed by gangs, and much more than that in certain large cities. Thus, gang violence is a major factor contributing to the high black and black homicide rate. Therefore, an approach of improving the inner city communities where blacks are concentrated and most of these homicides occur could help to provide a more realistic solution to reducing the carnage than solely placing the blame on racial bias by the police.

CHAPTER 7: HOW BAD ARE BLACK HOMICIDE RATES?

What is the relationship between homicide statistics and other factors, such as the state of residence, gun ownership, the percentage of blacks or Hispanics in each state, and the median income or incidence of poverty in that state? Homicide statistics are most closely correlated with the percentage of African-Americans in that state and with lower incomes, possibly because living in a lower income community can lead one into crime when jobs and money are scarce. Here's what I found.

The Major Correlations

- There was no correlation between homicide rates and gun ownership, so owning guns doesn't increase the chance of killing someone or being killed – statistics the gun lobby should like.

- Homicide rates for not only blacks but for all Americans are correlated with the percentage of African Americans in each state. Since homicide rates are highest for blacks, black homicides don't just affect blacks, but they contribute significantly (and disproportionately) to homicide statistics for the entire population. The similar number of white homicides don't factor into the comparison, because the proportion of whites in the population is much higher.

- There was a correlation, albeit a weaker one, between homicide rates and median income in each state. Higher homicide rates accompanied *lower* median income. A likely reason is that poverty leads to crime, since the criminals seek to generate income when jobs are scarce. Being impoverished can also lead individuals to turn to illegal means of making money, such as drugs. Then, engaging in these illegal activities can contribute to higher homicide rates due to the growth of gangs as business enterprises running these activities, especially selling drugs. A high crime rate might in turn contribute to lower income in an area, due to the flight of middle income individuals, both white and black, from a high crime community, contributing to further poverty and crime in these areas.

Correlations by state might also have regional explanations apart from the problem of urban violence, in that inner city homicide and crime rates are the highest. Donald Trump recently proclaimed that the African American community never had it so bad in the inner cities and that Democrats had done little to alleviate their plight, so what did they have to lose by supporting him? Though Trump convinced very few blacks to switch their vote to him, perhaps he did have a good point in that their situation was now so bad that something had to change for things to get better for them.

Since the data from the states does not distinguish between the homicide rates in inner cities and the rest of the country, I examined FBI and census statistics from 2008-2010 to obtain statistics from over 3000 individual counties nationwide. I assumed that counties with a population under 50,000 were rural counties and that urban counties had populations greater than 50,000. Since the number of homicides in many rural counties was zero, I used statistics on violent crime, including homicides, along with robberies, rape, attempted murder, and battery, for a comparison. The correlation factor "r" in a regression analysis ranges from 0 to 1, with a "no correlation" result being close to 0, a weak correlation between 0.3 and 0.5, a moderate correlation between 0.5 and 0.7, and a strong correlation reflected by an r higher than 0.7, with a 1 representing a complete correlation.

How I Made the Correlations

Following are some charts showing how I made these correlations, using examples from Ohio and Florida.

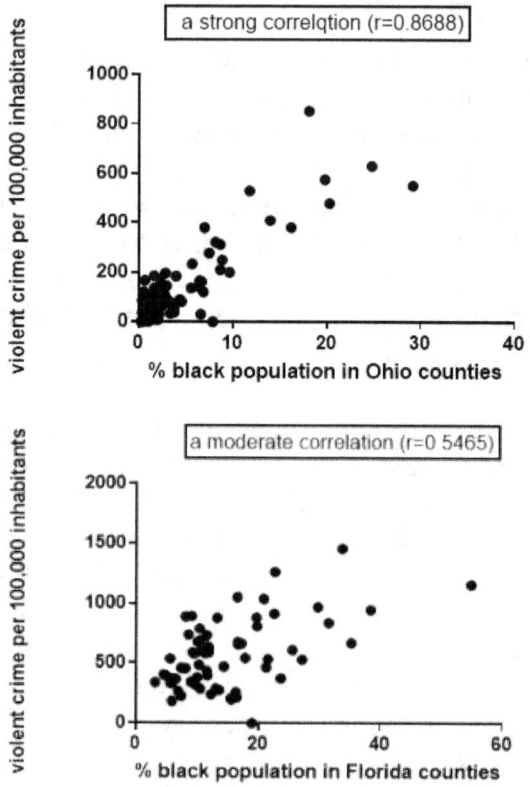

Other Correlations for Violent Crime Rates

Here are still other correlations I found.
- There was a correlation between violent crime rates and the percentage of black residents in each county in 39 of 50 states. Most of those states that failed to show a correlation had a percentage of the black population below the national average. Nine states showed a strong correlation between violent crime rates and the percentage of black residents, meaning that the violent crime rates were higher when the community had a higher percentage of black residents.
- Though there was some correlation, it was weaker in more rural counties with a population under 50,000, and less than half of the 44 states analyzed showed a correlation between the percentage of black residents and violent crime rates. Only one state showed a

strong correlation.

- The correlation between a high rate of violent crime and the percentage of blacks was stronger in urban counties with a population over 50,000, and two-thirds of the states analyzed showed such a correlation. Nearly every state that didn't show a correlation had a percentage of the black population under the national average. More than half of the states that showed a correlation showed a strong correlation.

What These Correlations Show about Crime

In short, violent crime and most probably homicide rates correlate highly with the percentage of blacks in the population, especially in US cities. Does crime lead to the increased urban black population? Or does the increased urban black population lead to high crime? Unfortunately, both factors are likely to contribute to what has become a downward spiral for our cities. Violent crime is likely to have caused an increase in the urban black population because it has led to the flight of middle class whites and blacks to suburban areas with lower crime rates. Though it is politically incorrect to say this, it is even more likely that an increase in the urban black population has led to more violent crime due to their higher rate of low incomes and poverty, in part due to their lower level of education, higher unemployment rate, and employment in lower paying jobs.

The high rate of crime, violence, and homicide does not seem to accompany middle and upper income blacks who move out of low income, high crime areas. Therefore, the increase in crime in predominantly black urban areas is probably due to the conditions affecting black lives, such as low income, impoverished families, poor education, poor housing, and living in an environment of gangs and drug wars, as discussed next.

CHAPTER 8: WHY ARE URBAN BLACKS ASSOCIATED WITH VIOLENT CRIME?

My first blog in this series determined that most blacks were killed by other blacks, far more than by police, and that blacks killed few whites. The second blog determined that gun ownership did not correlate with homicide statistics in different states, but that the percentage of blacks in the population did, and that the correlation of black residence with violent crime was strongest in urban counties. States with lower median income also had higher homicide statistics. Thus, there seemed to be a possible correlation between the high homicide rates of blacks and poverty.

To verify this, I looked at the overall poverty rates in different counties and the percentage of blacks below the poverty line in each county to see if these statistics correlated with the incidence of violent crime. To test this, I sampled 7 states with a black population over 10% and 10 others with a black population less than 10%. I used this 10% figure, since overall, African Americans constituted 12.6% of the populace in the US as of 2010).

Results of the Analysis

The results of this analysis suggest a strong correlation between violence and poverty in urban areas. Overall, it appeared that urban correlations in most states were stronger than rural ones, and correlations were similar for the incidence of violent crime among blacks and with respect to black poverty. In this mix of 17 states, I observed correlations with violent crime rates and black poverty in several categories in 14 of these states. While police bias might contribute to some extent to the high crime rate, due to a greater propensity to stop and arrest blacks, this bias cannot explain all of the correlations.

- In the 7 states with black populations over 10%, 3 states (Arkansas, Florida and Pennsylvania) showed a strong correlation between the black population and violent crime. This correlation was particularly strong in presumably urban counties in 3 states (Mississippi, Illinois and Texas), which showed moderate correlations. Only Louisiana failed to show any correlation between black residence and urban crime. Tellingly, the same correlations held up when comparing violent crime rates to the incidence of black poverty in each county's population.

- In the 10 states with black populations under 10%, 3 states (Kentucky, Minnesota and Oregon), showed strong correlations, and these correlations were stronger still in their urban counties, and I found similar correlations in comparing crime rates and black poverty. As I found, 5 states (California, Kansas, Montana, Nevada and New Mexico) showed more modest correlations, and only Arizona and Maine showed no correlation with either black incidence or poverty.

Reasons for the Results

What are the reasons for these correlations? Probably the most likely reason for the correlation of a high incidence of blacks living in an area with violent crime is the high rate of poverty. Many blacks left the South and moved north, most migrating to cities because that's where the jobs were. But there they had to accept lower income jobs because of their inability to obtain higher income jobs, due to discrimination, their lesser education or lower skill level. The cities were also quite segregated, which may have contributed to the prevalence of black on black crime. Another likely contribution to the correlation between violent crime and poverty was middle class flight from areas of high crime, contributing to increased urban poverty.

Undoubtedly, several factors contribute to the higher correlations of urban blacks and poverty. One consequence of segregation has been to generate black ghettos in certain inner city areas, made all the worse by high unemployment among young black males and the poverty endured by single black moms. It is highly unlikely that single moms are responsible for much of the violent crime correlated with the black community. More likely, the high unemployment rate of young black males is a much bigger factor. Still another possible contribution to the higher correlation of violent crime with urban black poverty may be that it is generally less expensive to live in the countryside on a poverty income than in a city, resulting in less incentive to commit crime to get money to support oneself or one's family.

Even if Trump may have been correct in his assessment about the continuing plight of the African-American community, it is premature to conclude that a law and order approach, such as using stop and frisk tactics, is the answer. Rather the solution needs to both reduce the factors contributing to violence, such as gangs and drugs, and strengthen the poor community by helping the unemployed or underemployed find better jobs in order to raise the income level of those in the community. Job training opportunities might be a way to do this, perhaps through the new infrastructure programs that the incoming administration is proposing to rebuild America. I will suggest other remedies in later chapters.

CHAPTER 9: REDUCING VIOLENT CRIME BY RELIEVING BLACK URBAN POVERTY

Since violent crime correlates with black urban poverty, it seems likely that more onerous police tactics to intimidate young black males will generate a pressure cooker situation that may easily lead to race riots and more fearfulness.

Thus, since young black males are the source of much violent crime, something needs to be done to reduce this. One solution is to get rid of the incentive to turn to crime by offering more job opportunities. This will require more job training. In addition, young black males must be given better role models than wealthy black athletes, drug dealers and pimps. Being an athlete offers an opportunity for only a very tiny number of individuals, and the other role models are illegal and not desirable societal occupations. In addition, these occupations will only provide a living for a very small number of individuals.

In my book *American Justice?*, I argued that the War on Drugs has been an unmitigated failure, that marijuana should be decriminalized, and that more emphasis should be placed on drug treatment. These strategies might help to reduce the underground economy in the black community, and it would certainly be better to have more young blacks employed legitimately than in underground trades.

The Role of Role Models

Unfortunately, many role models have proved to offer false hope. One former role model, OJ Simpson, imploded. Other black athletes have demonstrated terrible behavior toward women. Wilt Chamberlain boasted of his sexual conquest of thousands of women, and several black athletes have been in the news recently for abusing their wives. Bill Cosby, a former role model, who supposedly represented an ideal dad, has been exposed as yet another sexual predator. The black community is full of worthy black husbands and fathers that their sons should look up to, but often young males raised by single moms do not have a father figure at hand, and they become misled by poor role models, or peer pressure drives them to join gangs or go in other more rebellious directions.

However, inspirational models might help to guide them by giving them new hope. In the last fifty or so years, there have been two great marches of blacks on Washington. Everyone in America is familiar with Dr. Martin Luther King's iconic 1963 "I Have a Dream" speech to 200,000 marchers gathered at the Lincoln Memorial, which many whites looked on favorably due to its pacifist, Christian nature. This March on Washington for Jobs and Freedom, led by Dr. King, emphasized the need to improve black opportunity for advancement. Regrettably, this opportunity has not been realized so far. In 1963, the black median income was about 54% of the income of whites, and by 2014, it had only improved to about 61% that of whites.

Less remembered is the 1995 Million Man March organized by the controversial Nation of Islam minister Louis Farrakhan to urge African American males to take responsibility for their own society in a Day of Atonement. This march drew several times more individuals than the 1963 march, but it never got the same attention as King's march, due to white resistance to the messenger because of Farrakhan's association with Islam, whereas King was a Christian. Yet, as controversial as Farrakhan might have been, he called for blacks to take more action and responsibility for their plight rather than relying on whites.

In his speech, Farrakhan made these remarks which emphasize creating healthy, peaceful, productive communities and avoiding drugs. Here are some key quotations from his speech:

"We talking about moving toward a perfect union. Well, pointing out fault, pointing out our wrongs is the first step. Black man, you don't have to bash white people, all we gotta do is go back home and turn our communities into productive places. All we gotta do is go back home and make our communities decent and safe place to live. And if we start dotting the Black community with businesses, opening up factories, challenging ourselves to be better than we are, White folk, instead of driving by, using the "N" word, they'll say, look, look at them. Oh, my God. They're marvelous. They're wonderful. We can't, we can't say they're inferior anymore. But, every time we drive by shoot, every time we carjack, every time we use foul, filthy language, every time we produce culturally degenerate films and tapes, putting a string in our women's backside and parading them before the world, every time we do things like this we are feeding the degenerate mind of white supremacy and I want us to stop feeding that mind and let that mind die a natural death. Take this pledge with me..... I, say your name, pledge that from this day forward I will never raise my hand with a knife or a gun to beat, cut, or shoot any member of my family or any human being, except in self-defense. I, say your name, pledge from this day forward I will never abuse my wife by striking her, disrespecting her, for she is the mother of my children and the producer of my future…..I, say your name, pledge from this day forward I will not poison my body with drugs or that which is destructive to my health and wellbeing."

At the time that Farrakhan spoke, the condition of black Americans had not improved much since Martin Luther King, and it has not improved that much since 1995. Back then:
- Blacks had a poverty rate of over 40% and a median family income that was still less than 60% that of whites.
- Black unemployment was over 11%, and over 50% of teenagers over 16 were unemployed.
- Black males were being murdered at a rate nearly 8 times that of white males, and organizers believed that the government dealt with blacks with law enforcement techniques and with welfare programs that had failed the black community.

Unfortunately, these statistics have only improved somewhat since (8.5% versus 11% unemployment overall, 28% versus 50% for teenagers over 16, and a murder rate 6.6 times versus 8 times that of whites).

Some efforts to make changes have been little noticed by the media. A 20th Anniversary March in 2015, with participation by the Black Lives Matter movement, received less media publicity. Perhaps its title "Justice or Else" was too confrontational and outward-looking. Barack Obama attended the 1995 march before he became a Senator, but as President, he did not attend the 2015 march.

Some Conclusions and Suggestions

Thus, Farrakanh's 1995 message did not achieve its intended goal of producing a more peaceful, productive black community, just as MLK's dream had failed. Nevertheless, if black males took more responsibility for their own situation and eschewed other temptations, such as participating in an underground economy and taking drugs, the black community would be much better off. Accordingly, I suggest that future marches with a more Christian bent or other events around the country might be organized to encourage more individual black personal responsibility, and these could be led by black role models such as Colin Powell or President Obama after he leaves office. In addition, middle class blacks who have moved out of urban ghettos should be encouraged to help out their less fortunate brothers, the impoverished denizens of the communities they grew up in, again by serving as role models, big brothers or the like.

While black women do not contribute as much to crime, they do contribute to black poverty statistics. Poverty in the black community is influenced by the low proportion of dual parent

households. Since 70% of black children are raised by single black moms, that guarantees a dramatically high poverty rate. The War on Poverty initiated by LBJ in the 1960's has not helped.
Although it did provide a social safety net for impoverished single moms, those single moms became ensnared by the welfare system into perpetual poverty, and too few succeeded in getting work to better their existence while simultaneously raising their kids. Their daughters followed this pattern, which perpetuated the problem.

 Three things might help to get these single moms out of poverty. These are:

 - Subsidized daycare for working single moms could enable them to go to work.

 - Black women need a good role model, such as the very popular Michelle Obama, to encourage them to avoid the pitfalls of becoming single moms.

 - Contraceptive implants, which are safe, effective, readily removable, and last several years, could be used to reduce the rate of unwanted pregnancies for teenagers of all races.

CHAPTER 10: HISPANIC CONTRIBUTIONS TO VIOLENT CRIME

In 2014, Hispanics made up a larger percent of the population (17%) than blacks (12.5%). Is there a relationship between Hispanics and violent crime? Donald Trump seemed to think so, when he announced his Presidential Campaign in 2015. In one of his first pronouncements, he declared a need to build a wall on our Southern border, citing a vast influx of illegal Mexican immigrants, whom he characterized as bringing drugs and crime, as well as being rapists. Progressives, who now avoid using the discredited term of "liberals," raced to denounce Trump as a racist, pointing out among other things, that as many or more Mexicans were returning to Mexico as those still coming into the US. As previously discussed, Trump's statement that African Americans in urban environments "are living in poverty, your schools are no good, you have no jobs, 58% of your youth are unemployed" had some truth to it. In a previous blog, I pointed out that the murder rate in Mexico exceeds that in the United States.

So, is Trump's claimed association of Hispanics with violent crime real or just fearmongering on his part? To find out, I used the same approach of correlating the homicide rate and the percent of Hispanics in each state as I did for African-Americans in each state. But I found a much weaker correlation than for blacks. When I looked at the relationship between violent crime and Hispanics in all counties, I found barely any correlation. I then assessed whether there were any correlations within individual states between violent crime and the percent of Hispanics in individual counties.

What the Correlation Results Show

The results showed only a relatively weak correlation. More specifically, this analysis showed the following:
- Only 12 out of 34 states showed a correlation between violent crime and the percent Hispanics in a county (whereas 39 out of 50 states showed a correlation for blacks).
- Only 2 of those states (Nevada and Rhode Island) showed a strong correlation (compared to 9 states which showed a strong correlation for blacks).
- Surprisingly, among the border states (California, Arizona, New Mexico, and Texas) there was no correlation, except for a very weak one in Texas.

There is also very limited correlation between percent Hispanic population and violent crime, when I examined the larger urban and smaller rural counties separately. As analyzed:
- Only 4 out of 26 states showed a strong correlation in their urban counties -- Kentucky, Nevada, Rhode Island and Utah (compared to 30 out of 45 states which showed a strong correlation for blacks). Out of the 26 states, the correlations were stronger in the urban counties for Hispanics compared to blacks in only two states -- Nevada and Utah

- Only 8 out of 34 states showed a correlation in their rural counties for Hispanics, compared to 18 out of 44 states for blacks). Out of the 34 states, the correlations were only stronger in the rural counties for Hispanics compared to blacks in Nevada, Oregon, Texas, Washington, and Wisconsin.

There was also virtually no correlation between violent crime and the rates of Hispanic poverty in different counties in any state except for Maine and Pennsylvania.

Why the Lack of Correlation?

In summary, there is much less of a correlation between the Hispanic population and violent crime than is the case for the black population and violent crime, even in a state like New Mexico, where Hispanics make up over 45% of the population. Lesser Hispanic involvement in gangs does not seem to be the reason, since Hispanics make up a higher percentage (45%) of gang memberships than blacks (35%), even in cities. Perhaps Hispanic gangs operate differently from black ones and value Hispanic family structure more. Indeed, one likely key reason for a lack of correlation between Hispanics and violent crime is the strength of the Hispanic family and community, which has a strong Catholic faith and a commitment to hard work and getting ahead in life.

Thus, Trump may have been correct in some of his assertions about the plight of urban blacks, but Hispanics do not appear to be as involved in crime as he has claimed.

PART IV: HOMICIDE RATES AND DRUGS

CHAPTER 11: DRUG OVERDOSES VS. HOMICIDES

For all the concerns about the numbers of gun-related homicides, an even bigger villain is the use of opioids, which causes more deaths by overdose than death by guns.

In the November 4 issue of *Science* magazine, in an article "Pot and Pain", Greg Miller indicated that the epidemic of opioid overdose deaths has been increasing. In 2014 alone, 28,647 opioid overdose deaths were reported, 18,073 of them from prescription opioids, and reportedly, the numbers have increased since then. This serious problem was even raised as an issue in several states during the recent Presidential campaign.

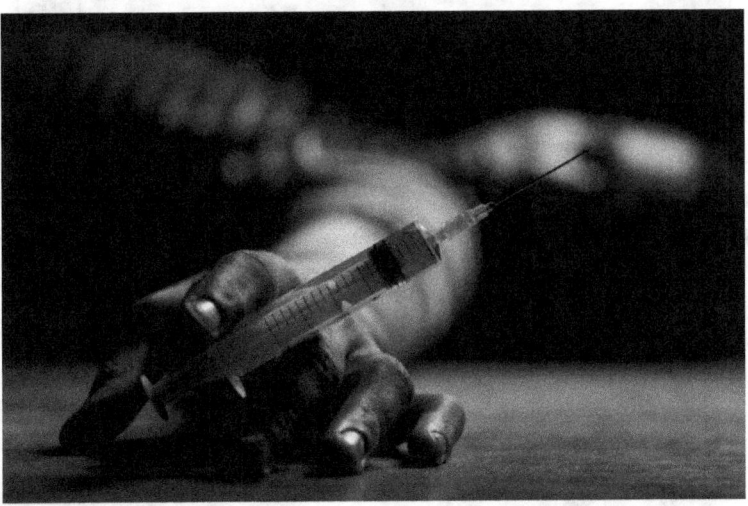

By contrast, compare those numbers with the 8600 gun homicides per year, as described in the first article in this series. Opioid overdose deaths are about three times higher. The numbers become similar only if one adds in the 22,000 annual suicides involving firearms, although most of the opioid overdoses were accidental, not done with any suicidal intent. Thus, even though both problems are difficult to deal with, reducing opioid addiction should be a priority, along with taking steps to reduce the number of homicides.

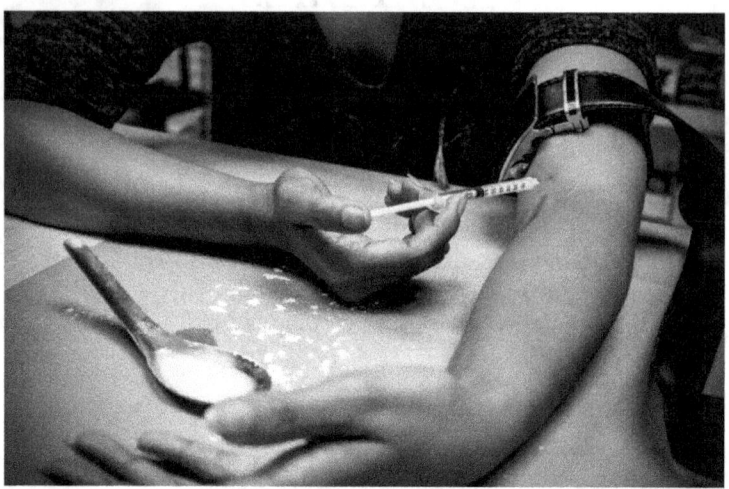

In his article, Miller pointed out that cannabis might be used as a painkiller alternative to opioids. The opioid death rate makes opioids a much more dangerous class of drugs than pot. After the most recent election, medical marijuana is currently legal in 28 states plus the District of Columbia, and its recreational use is now legal in 7 states and D.C. Pot is also not as serious a health hazard as alcohol, which at 88,000 deaths a year accounts for over three times as many deaths annually than opioids.

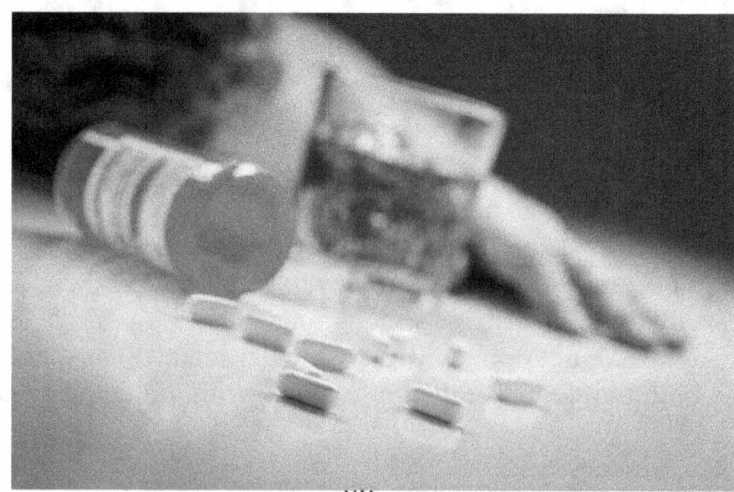

Nevertheless, marijuana use is still illegal federally and continues to be considered a gateway to other drugs of abuse. The Obama administration has not sought to challenge marijuana use in states that have approved its use. President-elect Donald Trump abstains from alcohol and all drugs that are considered addictive, but he has said he believes legalization of marijuana should be left up to the states. However, his selection for Attorney General, Senator Jeff Sessions, is a vocal opponent of marijuana legalization. Some members of Trump's transition team like Rudy Giuliani are known to be fervent believers in the War on Drugs, even though it has been very unsuccessful, as described in my recent book *American Justice?* Likewise, former prosecutor Chris Christie, another adviser to Trump, is opposed to marijuana legalization. It is therefore unclear whether a Trump administration will consider permitting federal marijuana use for pain as a means of combating the opioid epidemic.

Ideally, marijuana should be decriminalized primarily to reduce the huge numbers of individuals unnecessarily incarcerated for marijuana possession, as advocated *American Justice?* The possibility that marijuana could help cut down on the scourge of opioid overdoses represents a new argument in favor of its medical use.

    An irony in this debate is that the states' rights advocates are the liberal/progressives, in that 6 of the 7 states which legalized recreational pot and 20 of the 28 states which have legalized medical marijuana voted against Trump. On most issues, usually the conservatives are the states' rights advocates, while liberals/progressives generally favor federal rights.

PART V: HOW THE MEDIA DISTORTS THE NEWS ABOUT CRIME

CHAPTER 12: HOW THE MEDIA PROMOTES CONFRONTATIONS AND DISTORTS THE NEWS

I've been following the latest stories about the election and the news of killings of and by the police, most recently in Dallas, St. Paul and Baton Rouge. Unfortunately, the media has been treating the election like a prize fight, while painting a picture of a police force out of control and ignoring the good things that police officers do in their community every day. The net result is that the media sensationalizes the news which provokes confrontations (possibly sending the Dallas cop-killer over the edge), but ignores the policy positions of the politicians and the actual statistics of different types of crimes that should matter more.

These cherry-picked media stories thus can make a case much bigger than it is, especially when it comes to crime. These accounts thrust the victim and hunt for the perpetrator, if not already known, into a kind of mystery show that plays out in the news as long as there is new information and the public remains interested – until the next big crime story pushes it off the front pages.

As I have discussed in my book *American Justice?*, which discusses problems in the criminal justice system along with the story of my wife became a victim at the hands a hostile prosecutor, these big stories feature compelling victims, so everyone can feel the horror of what happened to them. For example, the stories may be about a young girl or hiker killed by a rapist, a husband pushed from a cliff by an angry wife, or a teenage girl who persuaded her boyfriend to kill himself by carbon dioxide in a truck. Such cases turn into tabloid fodder, though sometimes these stories reveal some misconduct by police or prosecutors in pursuing the case and turn into a call for justice.

Some Examples of Distorting the News

An example of distorting the news is the recent Steven Avery case, in Manitowoc County, Wisconsin, where the police or prosecutors might have planted evidence to convict Avery, who was previously convicted and later set free after DNA evidence revealed he wasn't the killer. Maybe things would have been different if Avery had simply gone on with his life, despite the injustice he suffered due to an overly zealous prosecutor who ignored witness evidence that excluded Avery as a suspect since he didn't matching the victim's description of her rapist. But since Avery decided to sue for false imprisonment and won a $36 million judgment against the police and city, he certainly made himself a persona non-grata in the county, where he continued to live. So, as seems likely to many commentators on the case, one way to make the suit go away was for the police to arrest him and the prosecutor to charge him and win a conviction against him for something else – the murder of a woman who came to the family junkyard to photograph a car. So now he is in prison while a new lawyer fights to free him.

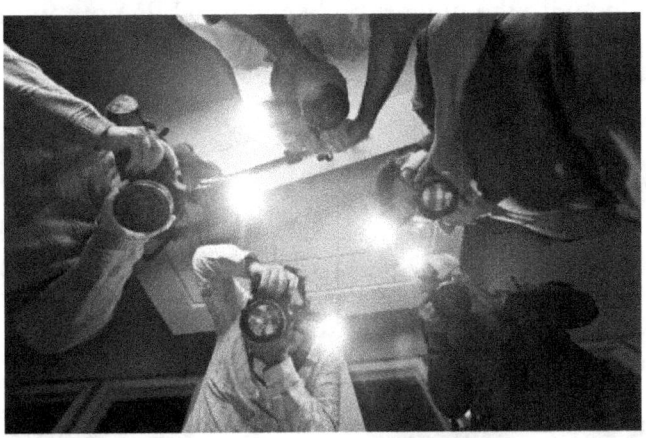

The local media originally helped him seem guilty, and then the Netflix TV series *Making a Murderer* helped to draw attention to his case, and the storm of protests led to a new lawyer signing on to try to reverse the verdict. I can really identify with such a story, since I saw first-hand how a determined prosecutor seeking victory can ignore the truth or not want to hear the other side of the story, if the truth counters a preconceived belief in the defendant's guilt. Then, the prosecutor may choose to accept the stories of one set of witnesses and not listen to the defendant's side of the story, which is what happened to my wife. The prosecutor chose to believe the lies of the kids who initially accused her of trying to run over one of them, a case bolstered by a hostile neighbor who claimed to have seen the incident, when any investigation would show he couldn't have seen what he claimed from his vantage point. But when my wife claimed this incident never happened, he ignored her entreaties, and the local media contributed to making her seem guilty as charged.

Another type of big story case now includes the mass murders of a half-dozen or more people in places around the U.S. – the bigger the body count, the bigger the story. All sorts of settings are fair game – from theaters and night clubs to schools. This is not to denigrate the seriousness of these cases, but to show how the media selectively picks a certain case to highlight – usually one with the biggest body count, while not reporting on the even much greater number of killings that happen every day due to road rage, family homicides and inner city killings of primarily blacks killing other blacks.

As with well-publicized cases of confrontations between blacks and police, such mass shootings are grim stories and need to be reported. But the media blows a selected case up out of all proportion to the thousands of other cases that have even more victims and are more common.

The Consequences of Misleading Media Accounts

Moreover, these media accounts have unintended consequences in creating other victims of hate. For instance, the mass killings have triggered a growing intolerance towards Muslim Americans, since two of the last killers had a heritage from the Middle East, though Muslim Americans have decried such killings. In fact, some recent killings of Muslims, such as a doctor being shot on his way to a mosque in Houston for morning prayers, are due to this incitement of anti-Muslim hostility. Cop killing cases have led to massive protests against the police and have contributed to a growing racial divide in America, since the police have increasingly been seen as the enemy in the inner cities.

Thus, the tension and the potential for even more conflict and violence continues, because these stories help to breed fear of the other and promote racial tensions between groups. By contrast, the truth is that most killings are due to conflicts with people one knows, and the statistics bear this out. For example, the majority of homicides occur between family members and between blacks killing other blacks. But the media plays up stories of the dangerous stranger, so fear spreads through the land.

Some Suggestions for Reducing Misleading Accounts in the Media

What is the solution to help reduce misleading accounts by the media or fearful impressions formed by the public? In *American Justice?*, I have made a number of suggestions to help overcome some key abuses by the media, which include making the defendant look guilty, notorious trial and pretrial publicity, racial basis, and criminal bias. For instance, the names of individuals charged with a crime should not be reported in the media. The media should not be permitted to write about what they learn from prosecutors, unless they also receive the defense attorney's comment on that information. They should stop hiding behind the use of the word "alleged", which readers basically ignore.

If false stories get published or produced, reporters, publishers, and others who have produced such stories should be required to do follow-up stories to make up for the false information that they have spread. Then, too, the media should not report speculations, rumors, and expressions of opinions as facts. Instead, they should be required to specify when they don't have actual facts in a case but are reporting rumors and social media musings. They should also direct more attention to the level of violence in our society, as exemplified by the number of individual homicides, together with suggestions for how to reduce it.

In short, I firmly believe the media should be held to higher standards of accuracy and civility, rather than sensationalizing cases to appeal to readers who want to be entertained rather than informed about the truth.

CHAPTER 13: WHEN THE MEDIA GOES TOO FAR: COVERING THE TRIAL OF A JUDGE FOR HIS CHILD'S DEATH

Another blatant example of the media going too far in sensationalizing a story occurred with the *Arkansas-Democratic Gazette's* August 14 to 20th coverage about the jury trial in central Arkansas of Judge Wade Naramore, also featured online at www.arkansasonline.com. A year ago, Naramore forgot that he had left his 17 month old son Thomas in his car, and the boy succumbed to heat stroke and died. He had thought he had dropped his son, who was in the back seat, for day care, but when he returned from his court hearings for the day and thought he was going to pick up his son Thomas to take him to a swimming lesson, he discovered the boy's lifeless body in the back of the car.

Though Naramore was devastated by the death of his son, sobbing hysterically and holding his son in his arms in his front yard exclaiming "I killed my child, I killed my child," as a neighbor reported, the local prosecutor charged him with negligent homicide. Though this charge is considered a misdemeanor with a maximum term of a year in prison and a fine of $2500, and Naramore was already wracked with guilt and grief, the media supported the prosecution in turning an accidental death into a media circus.

The *Gazette,* the biggest newspaper in Arkansas, headlined the trial on its front page and online for four days from August 14 to 20th, and the local TV media was out in force. So even though the jury ultimately concluded Judge Naramore was not guilty, based on his defense supported by an expert witness that he was so affected by other events that day that he believed he had already dropped off his son at day care. So he did not realize his son was in the car until his grim discovery.

Unfortunately, the media made the story as sensational as possible, appealing to the emotions of the readers, regardless of how much this would add to the deep suffering of Naramore and his family. For example, in an August 16 article headlined: "Attorney: Photos of Boy's Body Presented in Hot-Car Death Trial

'Made It Real,' the *Arkansas Democrat-Gazette* described in detail how "Naramore and members of his family could be seen sobbing at descriptions of authorities examining Thomas," and how Naramore at times "covered his face with his hands, unable to hold back audible crying." The paper also described how photos of Thomas's body were shown to the jury, as Naramore and his family continued to sob.

Then, in an August 18th article, headlined "I Freaked Out," Judge Told Police; Naramore on Video Details Events of the Day Boy Died," the press highlighted the contrast between what Naramore thought was a routine day of picking up steaks and wine, buying his wife a certificate for a day at a spa, packing a bag with Thomas' swimming gear, and calling his mother-in-law to say he was picking up Thomas to go to swimming lessons, before finding his body in the car. Moreover, the media continued to play up Naramore's continuing grief by describing how at each recess, he walked out of the trial arena to "gather his wife in his arms, rocking her back and forth as she cried." In short, the newspaper was doing all it could to paint a vivid emotional picture for its readers, using the pain of Naramore and his wife to make the story even more dramatic.

Worse, the media even played up an attempt by a detective to make it seem like Naramore might have forgotten his son because he was having an affair with another woman, though this wasn't true. For example, in this same article, after describing how Naramore rocked his wife back and forth to comfort her, writer Jeannie Roberts notes that "in the video of the police interview, detective Mark Fallis asked Naramore about rumors that he was having an affair at the time of Thomas' death." While Naramore denied the accusation, saying that he had "never even kissed" another woman after he began dating his wife, the paper printed this information as an innuendo, citing the detective as telling Naramore that he had the woman's name in his file.

At least the media did present the defense side of the case, pointing out that the detective lied about having the girl's name in his file, since he simply got an anonymous tip about her, and that he had discovered no evidence of infidelity. Also, the media did report that Thomas was well-cared for and that some of the defense witnesses had experienced leaving their own child in the car before quickly remembering the child was there before a tragedy occurred. Additionally, the media described at length the account of expert witness David Diamond, a scientist and professor at the University of South Florida, who conducted 12 years of research into why parents forget their children in vehicles – a phenomena due to various factors, such as sleep deprivation, a change in the usual routine, stress, or distraction, that lead them to experience a false memory of doing something that they usually do. So, as the media reported, Diamond gave an especially strong argument about why Naramore had come to believe he had already dropped Thomas off at day care that morning. Then, too, the paper described how after that incident, Naramore was inconsolable, had nightmares, and woke up screaming. Thus, it was understandable why the jury found him innocent, and why the courtroom broke into loud cheers and sobbing when the verdict of innocence was announced.

Yet, rather than briefly reporting the incident, the trial, and the results, the media turned the tragedy into a huge four day saga, which featured large photos of Naramore and his wife stoically and sadly going to court each day, much like they were on a perp walk, until the verdict of innocence came in. Then, the media featured a photo of a clearly distraught Naramore and his wife leaving the courtroom. Though he had been found innocent, the picture showed that they were both still grieving and devastated by the experience of both losing their son and going through the trial in the full glare of the media spotlight. In fact, the newspapers sought to prolong the story with its question for readers to vote on: "Do you agree with the jury's decision in the hot-car-death trial?" giving readers the option of agreeing he should have been found not guilty or of believing he should have been found guilty.

In short, the media had a field day in playing up the tragedy, the trial, and the Naramore's family's sorrow through a story to appeal to readers, while adding greatly to the Naramores' suffering. Part of the irony of the media pumping up the story is that the defense attorney maintained that no charges should have been filed. But whether these charges were filed or not, the media coverage would certainly seem to be excessive and did not really serve the public's need to know. After all, the judge was not going to be a threat to the public, since this was a tragic incident, where he already felt deep grief that he had killed his son. Moreover, his internal moral ordeal might lead to him becoming a more compassionate judge, should he encounter other defendants suffering great guilt and remorse over something they have done.

So why did the media make Naramore and his family suffer so much more? He had already suffered the greatest loss imaginable -- his only child – and making the loss even greater was that that the boy's death was a consequence of his own actions. As reflected in his repeated sobbing in the courtroom and his weeks of therapy, the guilt he must feel far outweighs any penalty that a sentence could have imposed on him. And his wife suffered incredibly as well from the loss of her child, all the more so by having to stand by her husband's side.

So why couldn't this horrific personal tragedy have been allowed to remain personal and private? Why couldn't an expensive jury trial with limited prosecutorial and judicial personnel have been better reserved for a felony case involving someone else with a more serious charge and longer sentence at stake? Or even if it was correct to have a jury trial on these charges, what good did it serve to so publicly rake this public servant and his family through the coals of media scrutiny, which could make this human tragedy even worse? Even if Naramore recovers from his self-inflicted psychological trauma, will his wife recover, and will their marriage survive? Will he be able to face community members after all this needless media attention? Will this cost him his career as a judge? He has already been suspended while a police investigation has been continuing, even after the trial has ended, according to media reports as of August 22nd.

In conclusion, the media attention in this matter cost this long-suffering family far more than even a guilty verdict in the jury trial would have. And this trial in the court of public opinion by the media wasn't necessary. It just appealed to the public's curiosity sparked by drama and excitement, but it did nothing to advance the public interest or the cause of justice. The members of the media covering the case were like vultures circling, waiting for the death of a wounded animal, or like the paparazzi harassing celebrities.

This subject of when the media goes too far is discussed in my book *American Justice*?. As the book suggests, it is time to rein in the media in their coverage of criminal matters, because they are not serving the public interest well by this sensationalized coverage that appeals to the public's baser sensibilities. Instead, the American media would do well to learn from the British system, in which there is a very limited amount of media coverage until an actual verdict is announced. Such an approach seems far more appropriate and humane.

CHAPTER 14: WAS THERE JUSTICE? THE RANGE OF ATTITUDES REFLECTED BY JUDGE NARAMORE'S TRIAL FOR HIS CHILD'S DEATH

At the end of August, the not guilty verdict in the Arkansas trial of Judge Wade Naramore for the accidental death of his child resulted in many impassioned responses pro and con about whether he should have been held accountable for this death or whether the jury was right to find him not guilty. One reason for the outpouring of responses was because of the wall-to-wall case coverage by the local media – but then that's another story which I have written about in describing how the media went too far in sensationalizing the case and causing Naramore and his family even more suffering than the guilt and grief he was already feeling. You can see my extensive discussion about the excesses of the media in my previous blog: "When the Media Goes Too Far: Covering the Trial of a Judge for His Child's Death."

Here I have asked the co-author of my book *American Justice?*, Gini Graham Scott, Ph.D., a writer, sociologist, with a J.D. from the University of San Francisco Law School, to comment on what it means to obtain justice in a case where an accidental death occurs. And when is one criminally responsible for causing the accident. These were the big issues raised by the case – both in the jury's verdict and in the extensive pro and con discussion as to whether the jury was right to find the judge not guilty. In general, most of the respondents felt the jury had done the right thing, and Dr. Scott would agree. But other respondents made a strong, compelling case for taking the opposite position, which might be appropriate under other circumstances, where the individual causing the victim's death is truly negligent due to his or her irresponsible behavior. But if not, the situation might best be regarded as a tragic accident. Let me explain, drawing on Dr. Scott's analysis.

An Overview of the Case

The basic circumstances of the case are this, as I described in my earlier blog. A year ago, Naramore forgot that he had left his 17 month old son Thomas in his car, and the boy succumbed to heat stroke and died. Naramore thought he had dropped his son, who was in the back seat, off at day care, but when he returned from his court hearings for the day and thought he was going to pick up Thomas to take him to a swimming lesson, he discovered the boy's lifeless body in the back of the car.

Naramore was devastated. He sobbed hysterically and held his son in his arms in a yard in front of his neighbor's house exclaiming "I killed my child, I killed my child," as the neighbor reported. So Naramore clearly had no intention of killing his son, and he had not engaged in any irresponsible, negligent behavior to bring about his death, such as being intoxicated, going on an extended shopping trip, having a conversation that lasted longer than expected, or meeting a mistress for some fun in the afternoon. Even so, despite this lack of intent and lack of irresponsible behavior, the local prosecutor charged Naramore with negligent homicide -- a misdemeanor with a maximum term of a year in prison and a fine of $2500.

Thus, under a legal definition of the crime, Naramore was certainly not guilty, as Dr. Scott points out. According the state statute, the state has to show "beyond a reasonable doubt that the defendant should have been aware of a substantial and unjustifiable risk that the death would occur." But in this case, Naramore offered ample proof that he was not aware, and as has been shown in many other cases, "simple forgetfulness is not a matter of criminal intent," as one *Arkansas Democrat-Gazette* writer, John Brummett, pointed out in an August 23 article, "Where We Go From Here After Wade Naramore Verdict?" which appeared the day after the verdict. As Brummett explained, the situation would have been different if Naramore had arrived at work that day, looked in the back seat ,saw his son, figured he was only going to be in the office for a few minutes and the child would be fine, but then the child died. Under such a scenario, even if he was gone only for that short time and did not get distracted by other events to say longer, he would have been guilty. That verdict would be the case, because he would have committed an unjustifiable risk providing the basis for considering him guilty of a criminal act. Likewise, if he had been drinking, and his reduced awareness caused him to forget his child was in the back seat, that would be another reason to find him guilty, because he would have been negligent because of his decision to drink and thereafter act under the influence of alcohol.

But in this case, Naramore had forgotten entirely because he was preoccupied with other ordinary things of the day, such as his upcoming court cases, his involvement in routine activities, and his feelings of stress. So he was for very good reasons not aware of doing anything that was a "substantial and unjustifiable risk;" therefore, legally he did nothing wrong. In fact, Naramore had the support of an expert witness who demonstrated that he was so affected by other events that day that he believed he had already dropped off his son at day care. His expert witness David Diamond, a scientist and professor at the University of South Florida, demonstrated this, based on his 12 years of research into why parents forget their children in vehicles. As Diamond explained, parents can come to experience a false memory of doing something that they usually do. In this way, Naramore had developed the false belief that he had already dropped Thomas off at day care that morning. And thereafter, he was truly devastated, had nightmares, and woke up screaming, helping to show how much he loved his child and in no way wanted to harm him.

Reactions to the Naramore Case

While some opponents of the verdict thought that Naramore's ability to hire an expert witness and lawyer for his defense enabled him to escape punishment, in most cases, as my co-author Scott notes, people aren't typically charged and convicted on the facts of Naramore's case, because simply forgetting something does not show criminal intent. Certainly, in a few cases reported in the news, the police have arrested a person for leaving a child in a car and charged them for being negligent, even when the child suffers no serious harm, such as in one case where a woman in Georgia stopped at a store to go to the bathroom and left her three young children in the car. Police officers arrested her when she returned to the car 10 minutes later, though her children weren't hurt. However, such an arrest is the rare exception, and Scott believes it is unlikely that the woman would be later prosecuted, though the children were released to their father. Rather, a probable outcome is for social services to step in to work out future arrangements with the parents to be sure the children will be properly cared for and safe.

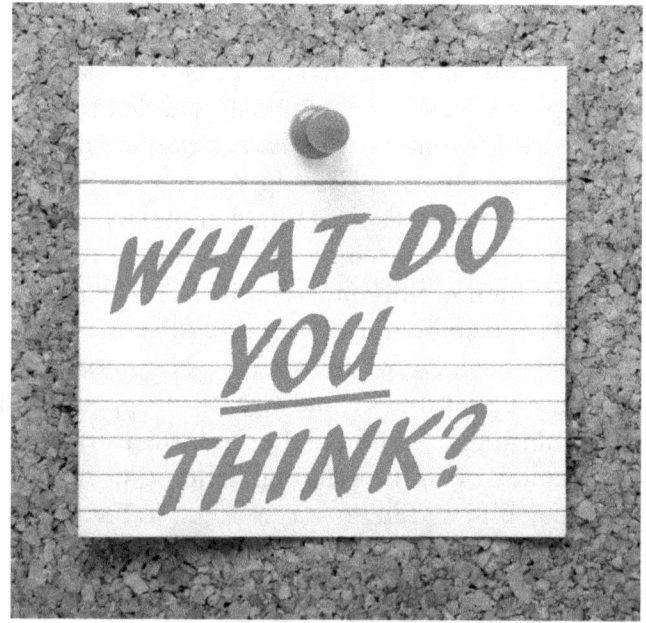

Thus, it is understandable why the jury found Naramore innocent, and why the courtroom broke into loud cheers and sobbing when the verdict of innocence was announced. But many others didn't agree, as reflected in the *Arkansas Democrat-Gazette's* reader survey of whether they agreed with the jury's not-guilty decision or whether they believed he should have been found guilty. Still more comments came in response to Brummett's article.

What is especially interesting is the way most of the comments did not respond to the legal definition of justice. Instead, those supporting the verdict tended to emphasize Naramore's great suffering and the fact that his feelings of guilt and loss would be much greater punishment than the actual punishment for the crime if he was found guilty. They also focused more on the judge's suffering rather than on that of Thomas, so they had more sympathy for the judge and his wife. By contrast, those who felt he should have been punished seemed to see this as a case of a high-profile wealthy person getting away with a crime because he could afford the best defense. The irony is that in actuality, Naramore was charged and went to trial because of his high profile, whereas if he was just an ordinary citizen, the police would not have even arrested him, based on the facts of the case, which showed his lack of negligence and intent.

To illustrate the difference, here are some quotes from people supporting the not guilty verdict based on focusing on Naramore's suffering:

"I fail to see what is gained by the State Extracting their Pound of Flesh from a Tragedy such as this. It does not deter, it does nothing except cause more pain and suffering."

"Of course the child suffered but at least he is at rest now. This man has already died a thousand deaths & will die thousands more in his lifetime. Nothing the court can impose could surpass THAT suffering."

"He will be living this hell for the rest of his life. Sympathy or hate is irrelevant – that is a fact. That will be his punishment, knowing that boy cooked while strapped to a death chair, under his care."

And there are some quotes mentioning the judge's suffering and lack of fault in making a mistake, thereby making a more legal distinction, without actually using legal terminology.

"Unless Naramore had been on drugs or drunk, he should not be prosecuted for this. This appears to be a case of negligence brought on by lack of sleep – not a more culpable state of gross recklessness…Accidents do happen. Unless the parents act recklessly, we do not prosecute. The death of the child is punishment enough. So sad…"

"There is no evidence of intent. No parent is perfect, and every parent has had accidentally done something that endangered their child. If this case was like one in Georgia where they clearly established that the guy was sexting and trying to get out of any unhappy life, I might believe he had intent. This case, however, is about somebody who was distracted and made a mistake. He will bear the consequences of his actions for the rest of his life, as will his family and friends."

By contrast, here are some quotes from the people feeling he should have been found guilty given the loss of his child's life:

"If this defense worse, then sad day for the life of a child …acting like it is just lost car keys with inconvenience of getting another set made…My real sympathy is still with the child."

"Not every law requires intent for you to violate it. So his lack of intent is irrelevant."

"Unfortunately FAIRNESS is an issue here. If the world were fair, no one would be blamed and jailed for an accident. But I think that we all know that that's not true. Had this been a minimal wage worker, working two shifts to try to pay the bills, truly overwhelmed by life, he probably would have gone straight into the jail before the funeral and would have been unable to attend his own child's funeral. I doubt that Naramore would have been very understanding with a defendant who committed such an act."

"He should have been convicted. That poor child suffered as his body temperature rose so high that he eventually died. How would y'all feel if this happened to your child at their daycare? You would want someone's head! No excuse for leaving your child to suffer!"

"The fact that Naramore suffered the punishment of losing a child should NOT factor into whether he is guilty of the law or not. It clearly did, however, given the verdict."

In a few cases, which I noted myself, some of those against the verdict felt the system discriminated against poor or minority citizens compared to wealthy individuals or those who are part of the system. They felt that Naramore got off because he was a well-known, well-connected judge. However, the irony is that he was actually charged because the incident gained a lot of publicity due to Naramore's position, and so the prosecutor felt compelled to charge him, though he wouldn't otherwise.

In sum, those for and against Naramore's guilt clearly had different views about what should be justice. Those supporting the verdict considered the judge's great suffering, along with his lack of intent and negligence, just as the jury did, while those who thought he should be convicted focused on the suffering of the child caused by his act.

ABOUT THE AUTHOR

Paul Brakke, is a scientist based in the Little Rock, Arkansas area. He became interested in studying the criminal justice system when his life was turned upside down after his wife was falsely accused of aggravated assault for trying to run some kids over with her car, since the kids and some neighbors wanted her out of the neighborhood. Eventually, they had to move, as part of a plea agreement, since otherwise, Brakke's wife faced a possible 16 year jail sentence if the case went to trial and she lost. He has previously told his wife's story in *American Justice?*, along with a critique of the criminal justice system. That book's website is at www.americanjusticethebook.com.